IT'S TIME TO LEARN ABOUT ANCHOVIES

It's Time to Learn about Anchovies

Walter the Educator

Silent King Books
A WhichHead Entertainment Imprint

Copyright © 2025 by Walter the Educator

All rights reserved. No part of this book may be reproduced in any manner whatsoever without written per- mission except in the case of brief quotations embodied in critical articles and reviews.

First Printing, 2024

Disclaimer

This book is a literary work; the story is not about specific persons, locations, situations, and/or circumstances unless mentioned in a historical context. Any resemblance to real persons, locations, situations, and/or circumstances is coincidental. This book is for entertainment and informational purposes only. The author and publisher offer this information without warranties expressed or implied. No matter the grounds, neither the author nor the publisher will be accountable for any losses, injuries, or other damages caused by the reader's use of this book. The use of this book acknowledges an understanding and acceptance of this disclaimer.

It's Time to Learn about Anchovies is a collectible early learning book by Walter the Educator suitable for all ages belonging to Walter the Educator's Time to Eat Book Series. Collect more books at WaltertheEducator.com

USE THE EXTRA SPACE TO TAKE NOTES AND DOCUMENT YOUR MEMORIES

ANCHOVIES

Deep in the ocean, small and bright,

It's Time to Learn about Anchovies

Anchovies shimmer in silver light.

They swim together, side by side,

A flashing school in the rolling tide.

Anchovies may be small in size,

But they are quick and very wise.

When danger comes, they dart and flee,

Moving like waves beneath the sea.

They have big eyes to help them see

Through waters deep and dark and free.

With tiny mouths, they munch all day,

Eating plankton on their way.

When the sun begins to set,

Anchovies dance, don't you forget!

They twist and turn in dazzling swirls,

Like sparkling ribbons made of pearls.

It's Time to Learn about

Anchovies

Lots of creatures love to eat

These little fish, they're quite the treat!

Seals and dolphins, big and fast,

Chase them as they swim on past.

Even birds will dive below,

Scooping fish up fast, oh, no!

Pelicans and gulls, so high,

Snatch them right out of the sky.

But anchovies play a special part

In nature's plan, a work of art!

They feed the ocean, far and wide,

Helping all life to survive.

People eat them, too, you know,

In tasty dishes, baked or slow.

On pizza, salads, or in a stew,

It's Time to Learn about
Anchovies

Anchovies add a salty chew!

So when you hear of this tiny fish,

Remember all the ways they swish!

Fast and shiny, smart and small,

Anchovies help to feed them all.

Now you know this ocean tale,

Of silvery fish that never fail.

Anchovies, swimming wild and free,

It's Time to Learn about
Anchovies

A little fish with a big legacy!

ABOUT THE CREATOR

Walter the Educator is one of the pseudonyms for Walter Anderson. Formally educated in Chemistry, Business, and Education, he is an educator, an author, a diverse entrepreneur, and he is the son of a disabled war veteran. "Walter the Educator" shares his time between educating and creating. He holds interests and owns several creative projects that entertain, enlighten, enhance, and educate, hoping to inspire and motivate you. Follow, find new works, and stay up to date with Walter the Educator™ at WaltertheEducator.com

www.ingramcontent.com/pod-product-compliance
Lightning Source LLC
LaVergne TN
LVHW052016060526
838201LV00059B/4059